LAUNCH INTO SPACE!

Exploring the SOLAR SYSTEM

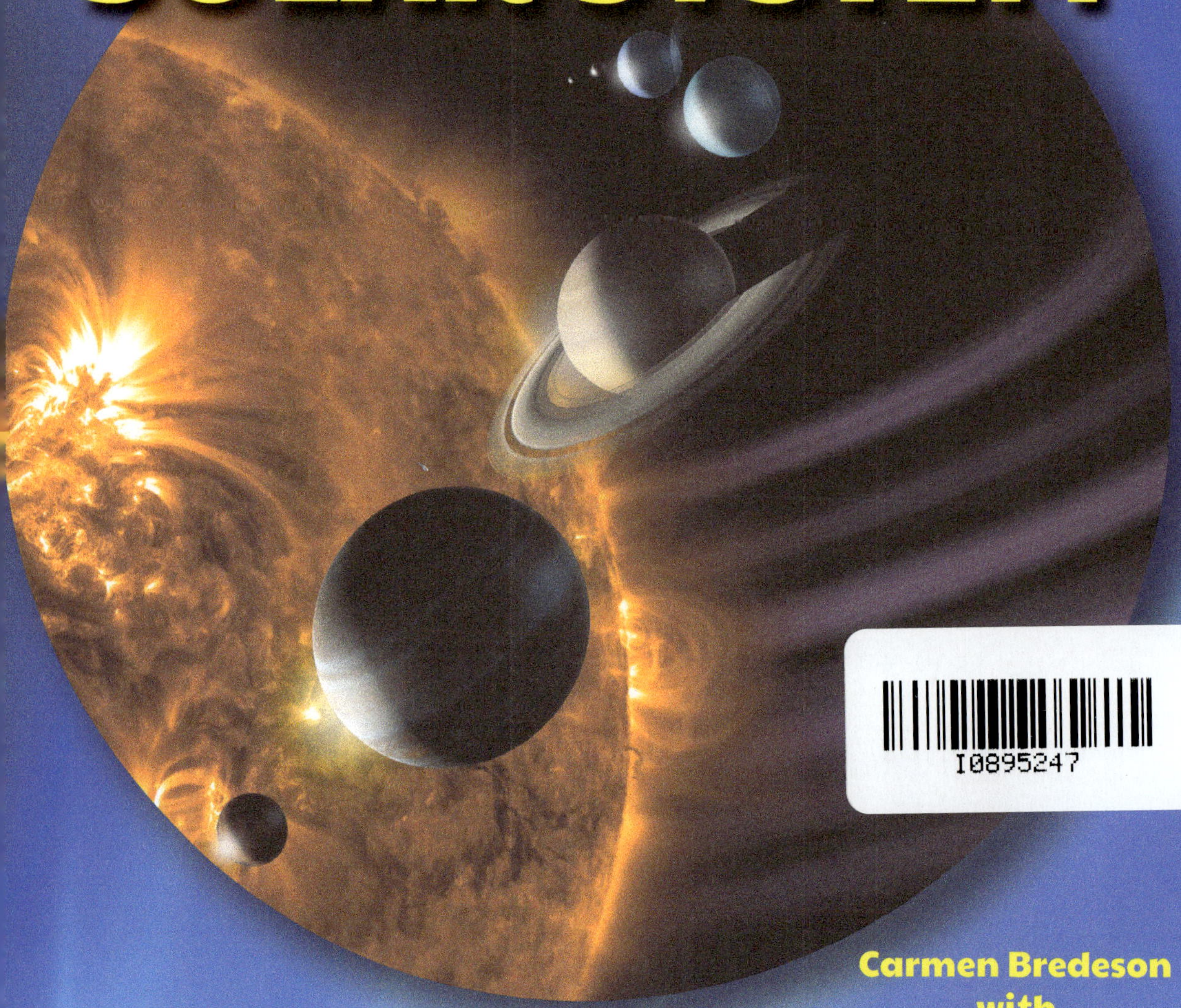

Carmen Bredeson
with
Marianne Dyson

Enslow Publishing
101 W. 23rd Street
Suite 240
New York, NY 10011
USA
enslow.com

Words to Know

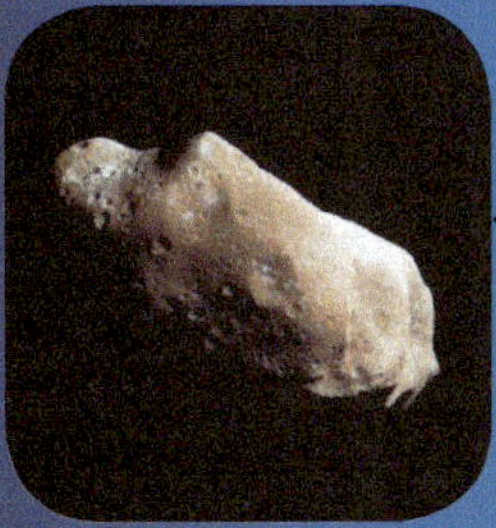

asteroid—A large rock that orbits the Sun.

atmosphere—The air around Earth.

comet—A big ball of dust and ice in space.

cosmic—Having to do with the universe.

dwarf—Smaller than others of the same kind.

galaxy—A very large group of stars.

meteor—A rock from space that falls to Earth and burns up in the atmosphere.

orbit—To move in an oval path around a star, planet, or moon.

planet—Any large, round world that orbits a star the way Earth orbits the Sun.

Contents

The Sun's Family

A solar system is a group of objects that orbit around a star. Our solar system centers around the Sun. The Sun is a medium-sized star. Planets, dwarf planets, moons, asteroids, and comets all orbit the Sun. Together they make up our solar system.

Cosmic Fact

Sol is the Latin word for Sun. *Solar* means having to do with the Sun.

A planet is a big round object that orbits a star. Earth is a planet because it orbits the Sun. The Moon is also big and round, but it orbits Earth, not the Sun, so the Moon is not a planet. There are eight planets in our solar system: Mercury, Venus, Earth, Mars, Jupiter, Saturn, Uranus, and Neptune.

Cosmic Fact

Our solar system is in a galaxy called the Milky Way.

The Eight Planets

For a long time, people thought there were nine planets in our solar system. The ninth planet was Pluto. But Pluto is smaller than the Moon. It is now believed to be too small to be considered a planet. In August 2006, scientists officially called Pluto a dwarf planet. A dwarf planet is similar to a planet but much smaller. Pluto has three moons. The largest one is called Charon.

Cosmic Fact

Like Pluto, Ceres and Eris are also dwarf planets in the solar system.

Moon
Eris
Earth
Ceres
Pluto
Charon

Mercury, Venus, Earth, and Mars are made of rock. Jupiter, Saturn, Uranus, and Neptune are made of gas. You could not stand on a gas planet. It would be like trying to stand on a cloud.

Cosmic Fact

Scientists have found more than five hundred other solar systems in our galaxy.

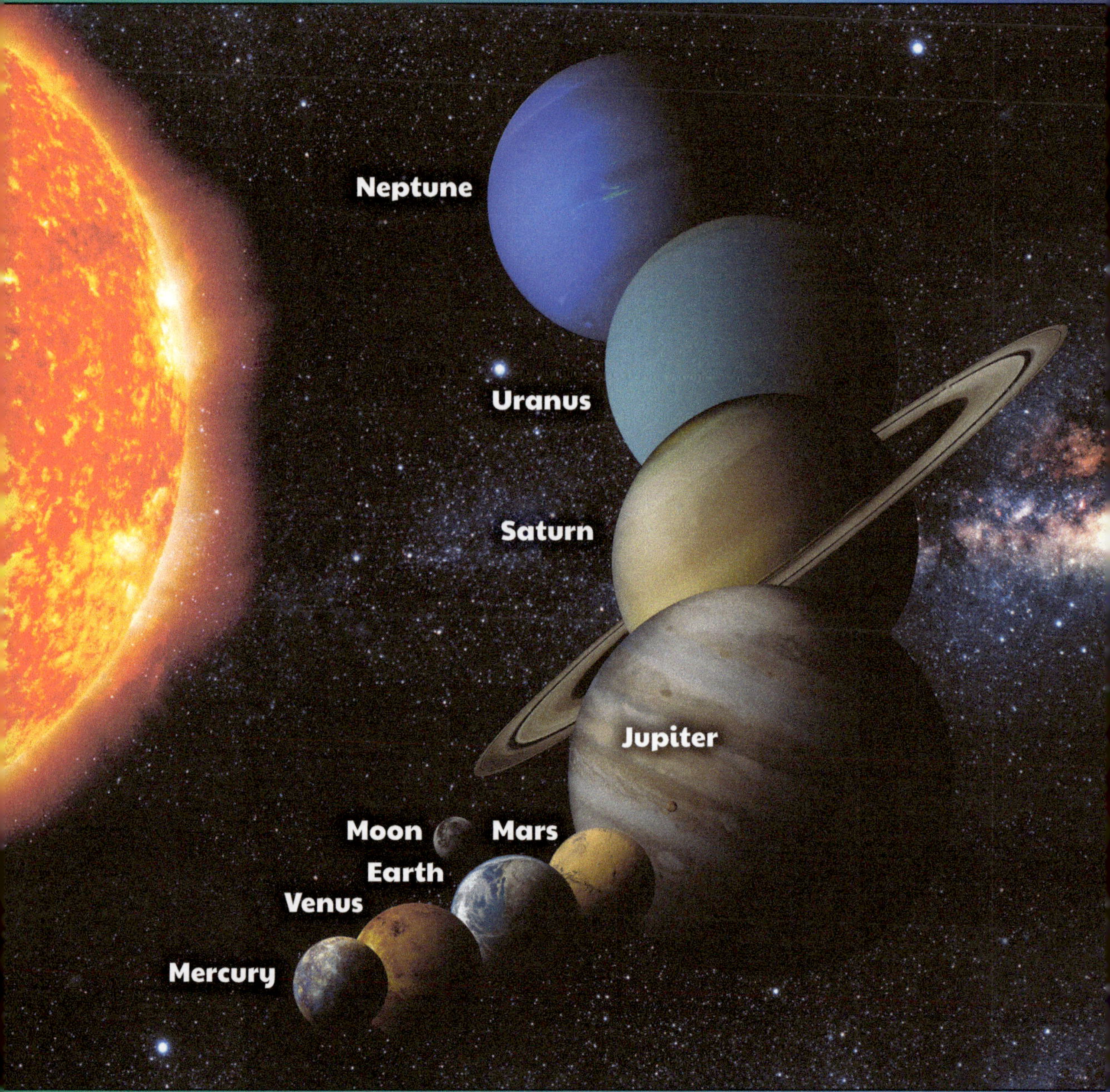
Neptune
Uranus
Saturn
Jupiter
Moon
Mars
Earth
Venus
Mercury

How the Planets Measure Up

Jupiter is the biggest planet in the solar system. More than one thousand Earths could fit inside Jupiter. Mercury is the smallest planet. It is the closest planet to the Sun, and it is very hot.

Cosmic Fact

Jupiter has a giant storm called the Great Red Spot. The storm is as large as three Earths, and it has been raging for hundreds of years!

EARTH
Great Red Spot
JUPITER

There are almost two hundred moons in our solar system. Earth has one moon. Venus and Mercury have no moons. Jupiter and Saturn each have more than sixty moons! One of Jupiter's moons, Ganymede, is the biggest moon in the solar system. Ganymede is about the size of Mars. It is one and a half times bigger than Earth's Moon.

Ganymede

Ice in Space

All four of the gas planets have rings, but Saturn's sparkling rings are the easiest to see. Sun shining on the rings lights them up. Saturn's rings are made mostly of ice. Some of the chunks are bigger than a house, and others are as small as a piece of dust.

Cosmic Fact

Scientists believe Saturn's rings are made of pieces of comets, asteroids, or broken moons.

Comets are big loose balls of dust and ice. They orbit the Sun far out in space. When a comet travels close to the Sun, it heats up. Some of the ice turns into gas and makes a long, glowing tail. Some comets orbit the Sun about every three years. Other comets may take thousands of years to go once around the Sun.

Space Rocks

Asteroids are space rocks that orbit the Sun. Although some asteroids are bigger than mountains, they are too small to be planets. Most asteroids are found in the asteroid belt. The asteroid belt is an area of space between Mars and Jupiter.

Cosmic Fact

An asteroid can have a moon too. The asteroid named Ida has a moon named Dactyl.

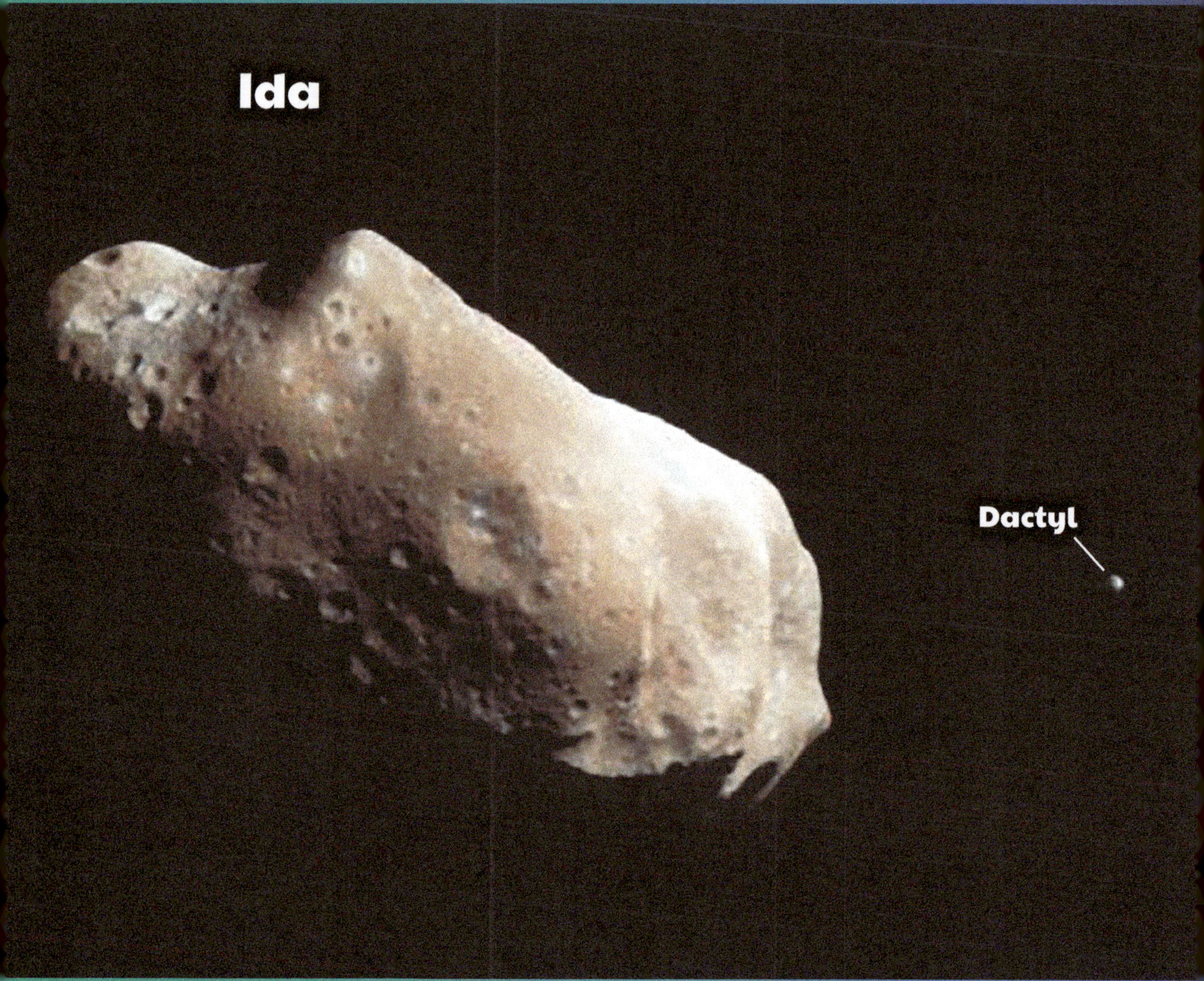
Ida
Dactyl

Some comets and asteroids lose pieces of rock and dust. These pieces zoom through space. A few of them reach Earth's **atmosphere**. Most of them burn up. These are called **meteors** or shooting stars. The ones that land on Earth are called meteorites.

This artwork shows a meteor entering Earth's atmosphere.

Beyond the Solar System

There are many objects farther out in the solar system. And scientists believe there are many objects that have not been discovered yet. One area of space past Neptune is called the Kuiper Belt. Scientists use powerful telescopes to look for objects in this area. Pluto, Eris, and other dwarf planets are in the Kuiper Belt.

Cosmic Fact

Objects in the Kuiper Belt are so far away that they take hundreds of years to orbit the Sun!

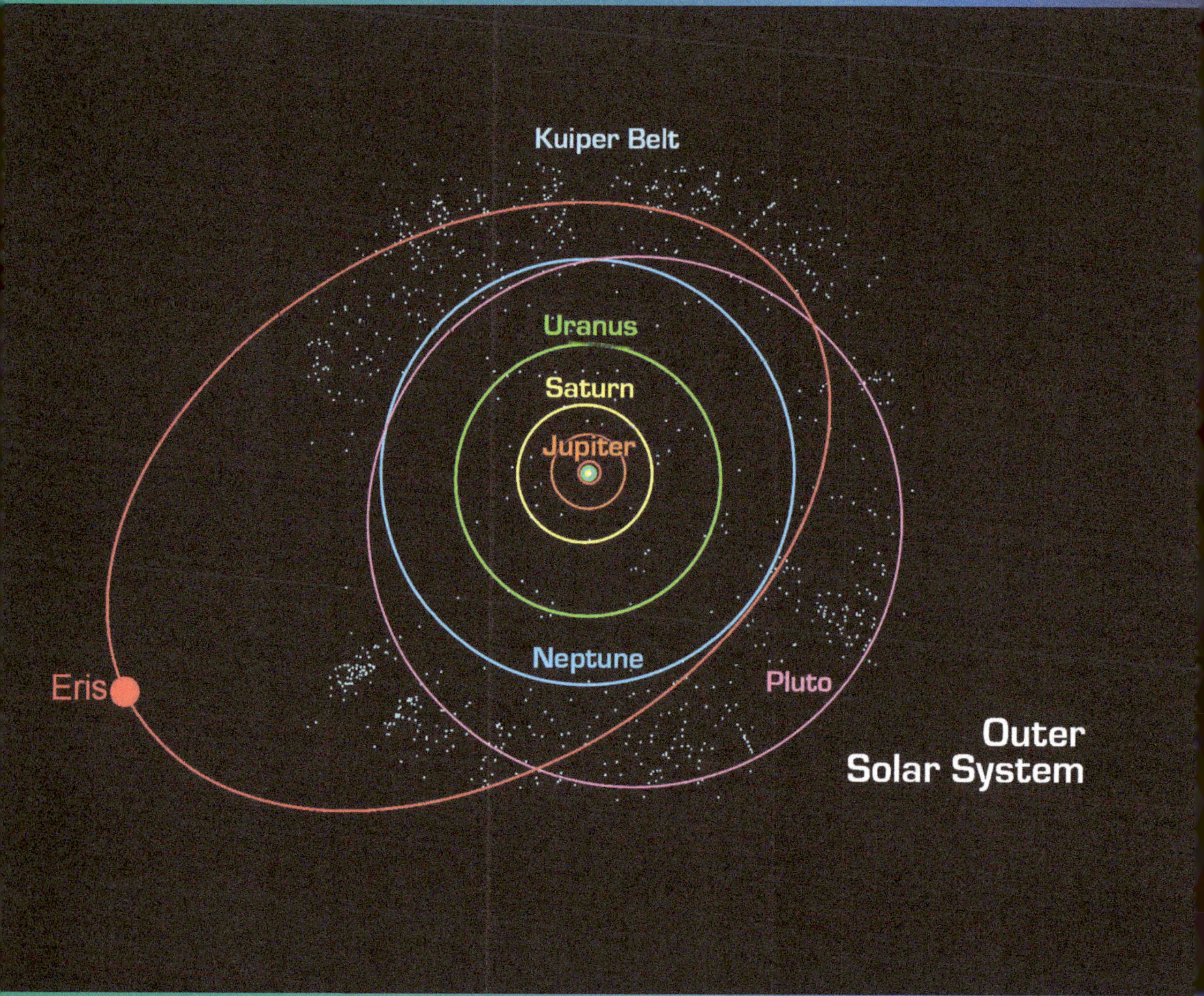
Kuiper Belt
Uranus
Saturn
Jupiter
Neptune
Eris
Pluto
Outer
Solar System

The Oort Cloud is a shell of frozen objects surrounding our solar system at the very edges. It is made up of about one trillion comets that circle the Sun in many directions. Scientists believe that the objects in the Oort Cloud are from when the solar system first formed more than 4½ billion years ago. Objects beyond the Oort Cloud are not part of our solar system.

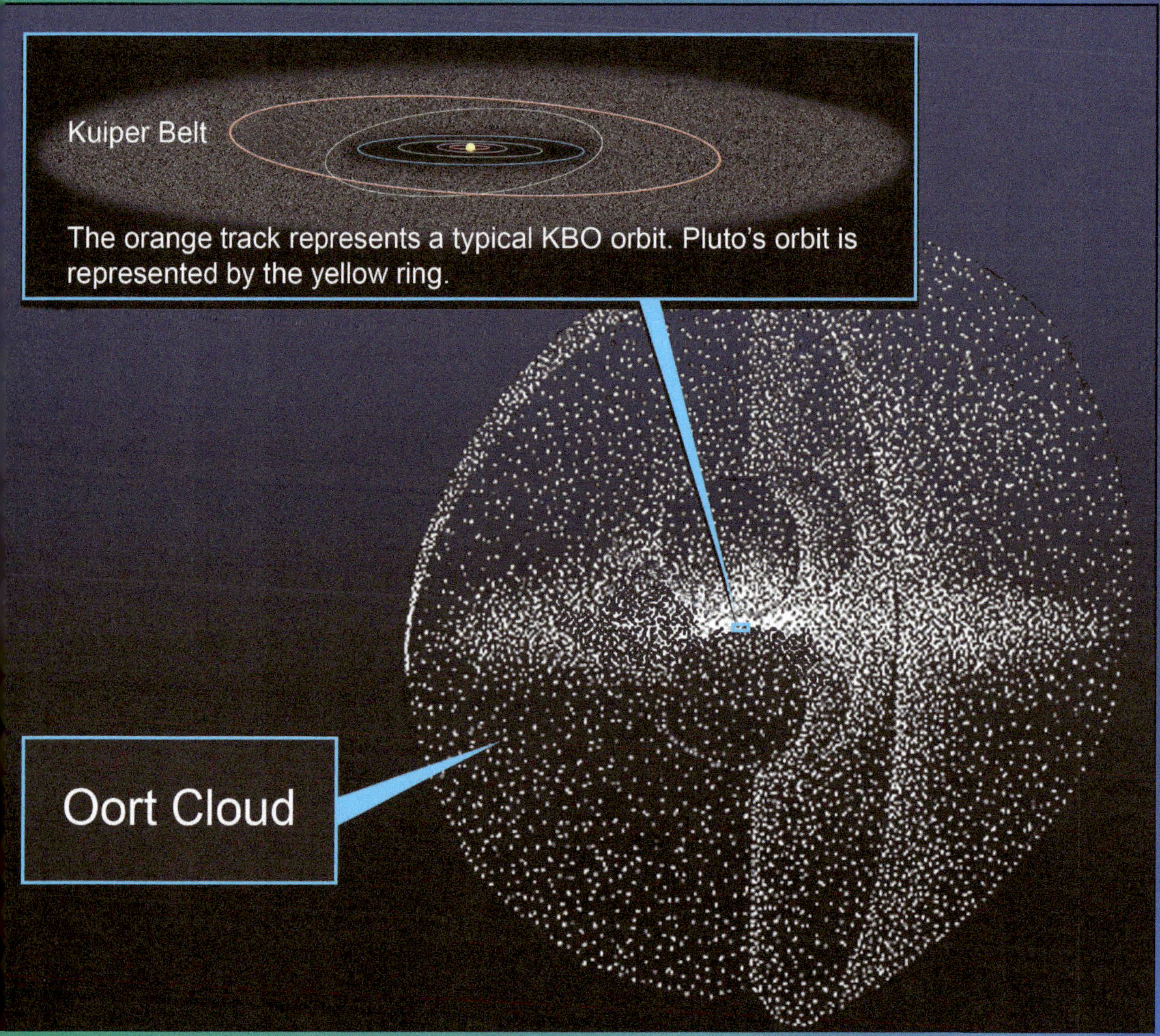

KBO stands for Kuiper Belt Object.

Earth Is Special

Earth's place in the solar system is just right for water to exist. If Earth were closer to the Sun, its oceans would boil. If Earth were farther away, its water would freeze. Plants, animals, and people all need water to live and grow. Scientists are looking for other planets that may have the possibility of life.

Cosmic Fact

Scientists think that Europa, one of Jupiter's moons, has an ocean.

Solar System Scientists

Many different kinds of scientists study the solar system. Astronomers use telescopes to study space. Mission controllers guide spaceships to the planets or into Earth's orbit. Geologists study what the planets are made of. Science teachers help students learn about space. Someday maybe you can explore the solar system too!

Learn More

Books

Branley, Franklyn M. *The Planets in Our Solar System.* New York: HarperCollins, 2015.

Higgins, Nadia. *Solar Systems.* Vero Beach, Fla.: Rourke Publishing, 2014.

Rustad, Martha E. *Space.* Mankato, Minn.: Capstone Press, 2013.

Web Sites

esa.int/esaKIDSen/Planetsandmoons.html
Learn about the planets and moons in our solar system.

kidsastronomy.com
Research resources, games, activities, and fun facts on the exciting world of outer space.

Index

Published in 2016 by Enslow Publishing, LLC.
101 W. 23rd Street, Suite 240, New York, NY 10011

Library of Congress Cataloging-in-Publication Data
Bredeson, Carmen, author.
Exploring the solar system / Carmen Bredeson with Marianne Dyson.
pages cm. — (Launch into space!)
Summary: "Discusses facts about the solar system, including the Sun, planets, comets, asteroids, the Oort Cloud, and the kinds of scientists that study the solar system"—Provided by publisher.
Audience: Ages 8-10
Audience: Grades 4 to 6
Includes bibliographical references and index.
ISBN 978-0-7660-6827-8 (library binding)
ISBN 978-0-7660-6825-4 (pbk.)
ISBN 978-0-7660-6826-1 (6-pack)
1. Solar system—Juvenile literature. 2. Outer space—Exploration—Juvenile literature. I. Dyson, Marianne, author. II. Title.
QB501.3.B737 2015
523.4—dc23
2014050370

Printed in the United States of America

To Our Readers: We have done our best to make sure all Web site addresses in this book were active and appropriate when we went to press. However, the author and the publisher have no control over and assume no liability for the material available on those Web sites or on any Web sites they may link to. Any comments or suggestions can be sent by e-mail to customerservice@enslow.com.

Portions of this book originally appeared in the book *What Is the Solar System?*

Photo Credits: Aleksandar Mijatovic/Shutterstock.com, p. 7; EpicStockMedia/Shutterstock.com (Cosmic Fact background); janez volmajer/Shutterstock.com, p. 11; MarcelClemens/Shutterstock.com, pp. 2 (Saturn), 17; Milanares/iStock/Thinkstock (blue/green background throughout book); NASA, pp. 1 (solar system), 3, 9, 25, 27; NASA/DVIDS, pp. 2 (comet),19; NASA/JPL, pp. 2 (asteroid), 21; Ralf Juergen Kraft/Shutterstok.com, p. 5; solarseven/Shutterstock.com, p. 23; Tristan3D/Shutterstock.com, pp. 13, 15; Willyam Bradberry/Shutterstock.com, p. 29; Zmiter/Shutterstock.com, p. 1 (rocket illustration).

Cover Credits: Milanares/iStock/Thinkstock (blue/green background); NASA (solar system); Zmiter/Shutterstock.com (rocket illustration).